# SUSTAINABLE
# LIVING

## BY HARRIET BRUNDLE

PLANET EARTH **HELPERS**

# BookLife
## PUBLISHING

©2020
**BookLife Publishing Ltd.**
**King's Lynn**
**Norfolk PE30 4LS**

All rights reserved.
Printed in Malaysia.

A catalogue record for this
book is available from the
British Library.

**ISBN:** 978-1-78637-995-5

**Written by:**
Harriet Brundle

**Edited by:**
Emilie Dufresne

**Designed by:**
Jasmine Pointer

# IMAGE CREDITS

*All images are courtesy of Shutterstock.com, unless otherwise specified. With thanks to Getty Images, Thinkstock Photo and iStockphoto.*
*Front Cover – Bukavik, sproba. 6 – KittyVector, matsabe, Visual Generation. 7 – Pogorelova Olga, Andres_Aneiros. 8 – Arcady. 9 – Pretty*
*Vectors. 14 – DeawSS, EniaB. 15 – Sergey Pekar. 16 – ideyweb, light_s. 17 – Maike Hildebrandt. 18 – natianis. 19 – iana kauri, Viktorija, Reuta,*
*VectorShow. 20 – Studio Photo MH, Jane Kelly. 21 – Oceloti. 23 – Incomible.*

# CONTENTS

Page 4     What Is Sustainable Living?

Page 6     Pollution and the Planet

Page 8     Your Carbon Footprint

Page 10     Travel

Page 12     Recycling and Waste

Page 16     Do It Yourself!

Page 18     Around Your Home

Page 20     Thinking Ahead

Page 22     How Can I Help?

Page 24     Glossary and Index

Words that look like **this** can be found in the glossary on page 24.

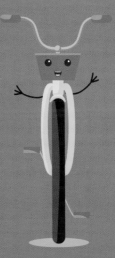

# WHAT IS SUSTAINABLE LIVING?

Hi, I'm Billy Bike.
It's nice to meet you!

Sustainable living is all about choosing a lifestyle that helps to look after the **natural resources** found on our planet, such as fresh water, land and plants.

To live a sustainable lifestyle, we need to look after or **replace** the resources we use so that they are there for the future. We can all try to make more sustainable lifestyle choices.

Hi, Billy. I'm Harry Helmet.

# POLLUTION
# AND THE PLANET

Many of our natural resources are being used without being replaced. Other natural resources are being **polluted**.

Some pollution is caused by burning <u>fossil fuels</u>.

Water and land around the world is being polluted by waste that is being dumped. Waste is being put into oceans and landfill sites. Landfill sites are large holes in the Earth.

# YOUR CARBON FOOTPRINT

The smaller your carbon footprint, the better.

Everyone has a carbon footprint. Your carbon footprint is the amount of **carbon dioxide** that your activities **produce**.

When fossil fuels are burned, carbon dioxide is released. Every time you do something that produces carbon dioxide, it adds to your carbon footprint.

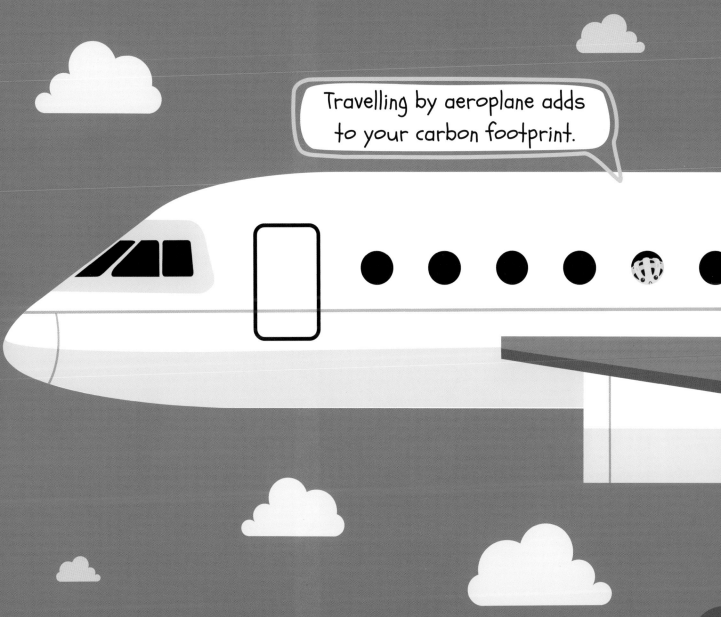

Travelling by aeroplane adds to your carbon footprint.

# TRAVEL

You can help to reduce your carbon footprint by thinking about how you travel. Some vehicles, such as cars, burn fossil fuels. This creates pollution and adds to your carbon footprint.

I don't create any pollution.

To make a more sustainable choice, you could walk or cycle to where you're going. If you're going on a longer journey, speak to an adult about **car sharing** or using public transport.

When you cycle, don't forget to put me on to be safe!

# RECYCLING AND WASTE

Don't throw Billy away!

Have you ever thought about where the things you throw away end up? What we throw away might be taken to landfill sites, be burned or be dumped into water. These all cause pollution.

Try to buy things that have no packaging and recycle things when possible. Recycling is when an item is made into something which can be used again rather than thrown away.

Plastic items can take hundreds of years to break down and are particularly harmful to the planet. Single-use plastics are plastic items that are only used once before being thrown away.

Single-use plastics create lots of waste in the world.

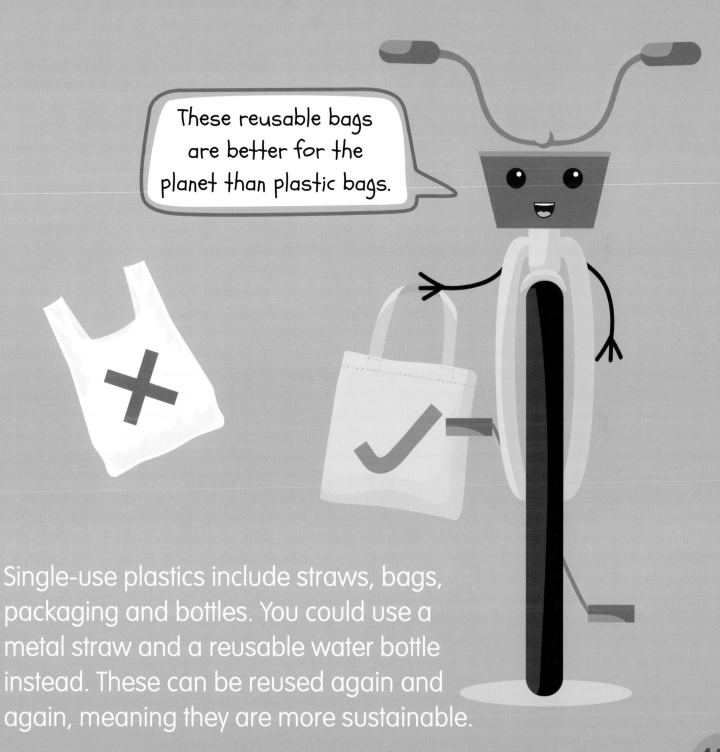

Single-use plastics include straws, bags, packaging and bottles. You could use a metal straw and a reusable water bottle instead. These can be reused again and again, meaning they are more sustainable.

# DO IT YOURSELF!

The food we buy in supermarkets usually causes pollution in some way. This pollution might come from how the food is grown, packaged or **transported**.

This lorry transporting food is causing pollution.

You could try to grow your own food! Speak to an adult about setting up a vegetable patch in your garden or at school. You could grow potatoes, tomatoes, carrots and lots of other delicious foods.

Certain times of year are best for planting. Ask an adult to help you get it right.

# AROUND YOUR HOME

Lots of the things in our homes use the planet's natural resources. There are many small changes we can easily make to help us live more sustainable lifestyles.

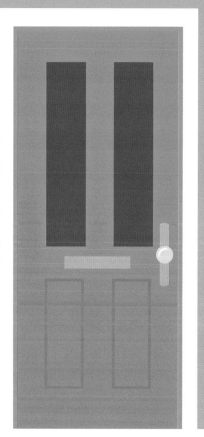

Think about all the things you use around your home. What changes could you make?

Make sure your devices are not left on standby, because this uses energy.

Turn off the lights when you leave a room. This saves energy.

ON

OFF

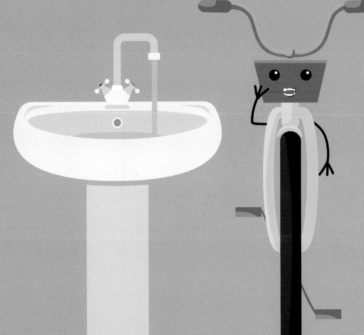

Don't leave the tap running while you brush your teeth. This helps to save water.

Turn off the tap, Billy!

# THINKING AHEAD

I'm thirsty!

If we don't start to look after our planet, we could cause damage that cannot be **reversed**. Air pollution could cause people to become very ill and water pollution could mean we run out of fresh water.

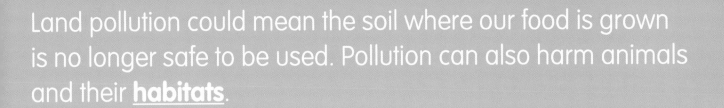

Land pollution could mean the soil where our food is grown is no longer safe to be used. Pollution can also harm animals and their **habitats**.

Pollution helps to cause **climate change**, which is very bad for our planet.

# HOW CAN I HELP?

Each person can make more sustainable choices. Try using the suggestions in this book to help you lead a more sustainable life.

You could put on a helmet and use a bicycle more!

People around the world are trying to reduce the amount of pollution in the world.

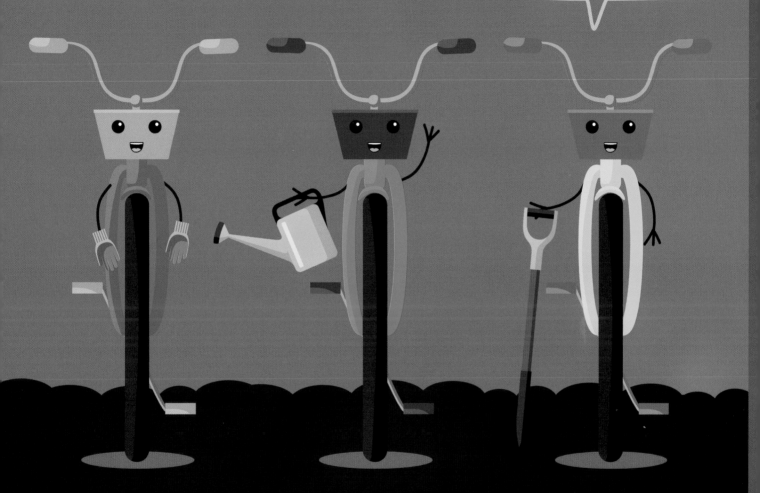

You could start your own **conservation group**!

Conservation groups are working hard to look after habitats and animals which are at risk, in order to help keep them safe.

# GLOSSARY

| | |
|---|---|
| **CAR SHARING** | using the same car as someone who is travelling to the same place or going on a similar journey as you |
| **CARBON DIOXIDE** | a natural gas found in the air that contributes to climate change and the pollution of the planet |
| **CLIMATE CHANGE** | a change in the typical weather or temperature of a large area |
| **CONSERVATION GROUP** | an organisation that helps to protect the planet |
| **FOSSIL FUELS** | fuels, such as coal, oil and gas, which formed millions of years ago from the remains of animals and plants |
| **HABITATS** | the natural homes in which animals, plants and other living things live |
| **NATURAL RESOURCES** | useful materials that are created by nature |
| **POLLUTED** | when harmful and poisonous things have been added to the environment |
| **PRODUCE** | make or create |
| **REPLACE** | put back what has been used |
| **REVERSED** | put back to how it was before |
| **TRANSPORTED** | carried from one place to another |

# INDEX

**AIR** 20

**FOOD** 16–17, 21

**LAND** 4, 7, 21

**LANDFILLS** 7, 12

**PLANET** 4, 14–15, 18, 20–21

**PLASTIC** 14–15

**POLLUTION** 6–7, 10, 12, 16, 20–21, 23

**WASTE** 7, 13–14

**WATER** 4, 7, 12, 15, 19–20